ASTROLOGY GEMS

ARIES
March 21 – April 19

Monte Farber & Amy Zerner

Sterling Publishing Co., Inc.
New York

Text © 2006 by Monte Farber
Art © 2006 by Amy Zerner

10 9 8 7 6 5 4 3 2 1

Published by Sterling Publishing Co., Inc.
387 Park Avenue South, New York, NY 10016

Distributed in Canada by Sterling Publishing
c/o Canadian Manda Group, 165 Dufferin Street
Toronto, Ontario, Canada M6K 3H6

Distributed in the United Kingdom by GMC
Distribution Services
Castle Place, 166 High Street, Lewes, East Sussex,
England BN7 1XU

Distributed in Australia by Capricorn Link (Australia)
Pty. Ltd.
P.O. Box 704, Windsor, NSW 2756, Australia

Printed in China

Sterling ISBN-13: 978-1-4027-4176-0
        ISBN-10: 1-4027-4176-6

For information about custom editions, special sales,
premium and corporate purchases, please contact
Sterling Special Sales Department at 800-805-5489 or
specialsales@sterlingpub.com.

What's Your Sign?

When someone asks you "What's your sign?" you know what that person really means is "What's your astrological sign?" Professional astrologers more often use the phrase "Sun sign," a term reflecting the concept that a person's sign is determined by which of the twelve signs of the zodiac the Sun appeared to be passing through at the moment she was born. The zodiac is the narrow band of sky circling the Earth's equator through which the Sun, the Moon, and the planets appear to move when viewed by us here on Earth.

Astrology's Gift

Astrology, which has been around for thousands of years, is the study of how planetary positions relate to earthly events and people. Its long and rich history has resulted in a wealth of philosophical and psychological wisdom, the basic concepts of which we are going to share with you in the pages of this book. As the Greek philosopher Heracleitus (c. 540–c. 480 BCE) said, "Character is destiny." Who you are—complete with all of your goals, tendencies, habits, virtues, and vices—will determine how you act and react, thereby creating your life's destiny. Like astrology itself, our Astrology Gems series is designed to help you to better know yourself and those you care about. You will then be better able to use your free will to shape your life to your liking.

Does Astrology Work?

Many people rightly question how astrology can divide humanity into twelve Sun signs and make predictions that can be correct for everyone of the same sign. The simple answer is that it cannot do that—that's newspaper astrology, entertaining but not the real thing. Rather, astrology can help you understand your strengths and weaknesses so that you can better accept yourself as you are and use your strengths to compensate for your weaknesses. Real astrology is designed to help you to become yourself fully.

Remember, virtually all the music in the history of Western music has been composed using variations of the same twelve notes. Similarly, the twelve Sun signs of astrology are basic themes rich with meaning that each of us expresses differently to create and respond to the unique opportunities and challenges of our life.

ARIES

March 21–April 19

Planet
Mars

Element
Fire

Quality
Cardinal

Day
Tuesday

Season
spring

Colors
red (all shades)

Plants
red poppy, thistle, ginger

Perfume
frankincense

Gemstones
bloodstone, garnet, red jasper,
fire opal

Metal
iron

Personal qualities
Honest, brave, and headstrong

We call the following words "keywords" because they can help you unlock the core meaning of the astrological sign of Aries. Each keyword represents issues and ideas that are of supreme importance and prominence in the lives of people born with Aries as their Sun sign. You will usually find that every Aries embodies at least one of these keywords in the way she makes a living:

initiation · challenge
adventure · exploration
daring · courage · honesty
competition · innocence
action · aggression · energy
spontaneity · discovery
creativity

Aries' Symbolic Meaning

The first day of spring marks the beginning of the sign Aries, the symbol of which is the Ram. Each spring, the desire to mate and stake his claim to his territory drives the ram to display his fitness and bravery by butting heads with his competitors. After a few times, the one who can handle the headache and hasn't given up is the winner.

People born under the sign of Aries have a lot in common with their symbol, the Ram. They are willing to butt heads with those they think are standing in their way. Brave and headstrong, they approach matters directly and forcefully. They're always striving to get the job done quickly, and they hate deceit so much that they can sometimes be too honest for their own good.

Aries is the first sign of the zodiac, and Arians, as children of Aries are called, try to be the first in some way. They want to be independent and original. They don't like to be second or even to wait terribly long for anyone or anything, and this can make them seem impatient and aggressive if they don't get their way. They function best when they act on their first impulse and don't second-guess themselves. They value strength, survival, and the kind of vital, unstoppable nature that enables the early spring flowers to push their heads up through the hard wintered soil.

Aries is one of four Cardinal signs in the zodiac (the other three being Cancer, Libra, and Capricorn). The first day of each of these signs marks the change of season. This is why the Cardinal signs symbolize forward movement. People born during one of the Cardinal signs tend to be goal-oriented, active, enthusiastic, motivated, and ambitious individuals who initiate change and get things moving.

Aries is also one of three Fire signs (the other two being Leo and Sagittarius). People with lots of fire in their chart are active, spontaneous, enthusiastic, creative, self-sufficient, and romantic. This forceful Fire element can sometimes make an Aries too proud, bossy, or pushy, but such an individual is just expressing life's vitality and usually means no harm.

Arians often get into trouble for acting without any forethought or consideration of others. But their self-reliant personality helps them thrive when they are in charge or working alone. Their fiery, assertive, and courageous nature is always charming and charismatic.

Recognizing an Aries

People who exhibit the physical characteristics distinctive of the sign Aries have strong facial features, often with piercing eyes. Frequently dressing in original styles and bold colors, they know how to look their best. Their bodies are strong, and they walk with determination. Vital and energetic, they project an aura of pure sexiness.

Aries' Typical Behavior and Personality Traits

❀ willful and bossy

❀ daring

❀ moves forward, even if afraid

❀ direct, open, and honest

❀ gets things done quickly

❀ highly competitive, hating to lose

❀ self-assured

- ✳ adventurous and enterprising
- ✳ enthusiastic and optimistic
- ✳ possesses very clear goals
- ✳ likes to get her way

What Makes an Aries Tick?

More afraid of being afraid than of anything else, Arians are always trying to prove how brave they are. Arians must remember that fear and self-doubt are not signs of weakness or losing control; nor are they a guarantee of failure.

The "fight or flight" instinct is a basic characteristic of Arians. If an Aries feels even slightly afraid, the emotion makes him either lash out or panic. Rams must stay spontaneous and not let their fear cause self-defeating behavior or paralyze them into inaction and cause even more self-doubt.

The Aries Personality Expressed Positively

Aries who are driven to push the boundaries of their chosen passion display the self-reliant, confident, and resourceful personality of their sign. They realize that they are on their own, but that that is a good thing, as it motivates them to be a shining example of what it means to be your own person.

On a Positive Note

Aries displaying the positive characteristics associated with their sign also tend to be:

* action oriented, taking charge of situations

* energetic and enthusiastic

* inclined to engage in networking

* vivacious

* positive

* heroic

* guileless

* passionate

The Aries Personality Expressed Negatively

Aries who boss others around and seem to believe that they have no faults display the self-limiting tendencies of their sign. Their desire to get the job done well and quickly may cause them to treat others as lesser beings, especially those they fear may not be up to the task at hand. Aries need to be aware of their human frailties without thinking they are "bad" for having them.

Negative Traits

Aries displaying the negative characteristics associated with their sign also tend to be:

* jealous and intolerant

* recklessly impulsive

* bossy

* defiant

* immature

* insensitive

* thoughtless

* too honest

* quick to quit

Ask an Aries If...

Ask an Aries if you want to know how to achieve your goals. He'll tell you what you should be doing and how you should be doing it. Just remember that he'll also tell you if your goal is not achievable, so don't ask if you can't take hearing the honest truth. Knowing an Aries is like having your own military general on call, always ready, willing, and able to help you plan your campaign. Just make sure you're ready to work until you drop.

Aries As Friends

Arians make for fun and entertaining friends, but they are not usually interested in entertaining for its own sake; they usually have a reason for having a dinner party or gathering. They like to network and meet new people who might be interested in their work or ideas. Aries friendships don't last long if the other party doesn't understand that the Aries individual is highly competitive and focused on achievements and furthering her career.

Arians make friends with original thinkers, especially those wise enough to recognize their uniqueness. Arians are warm and giving when they feel understood, but can be snappish if they feel threatened or misunderstood. However, a person who will support an Aries friend can enjoy an enduring friendship.

Looking for Love

Arians like to make the first move, and they are usually not afraid to do so. Even if they are scared, they'll still make their move—and be quick about it. They won't wait for anyone or anything. Arians must be assertive in their relationships.

An Aries needs to be with someone who is as alive and ardent as he is, or so appreciative of his energetic approach to living that it makes the Aries flame burn even brighter. Arians want people to respond to them in a real and honest way, and they like to test people by seeing how they react to Arian directness. While Arians may seem disinterested and contradictory, they're just trying to determine who a person really is.

If rebuffed, an Aries will move on without another thought wasted on the person who rejected her. It's rare to find an Aries feeling the pangs of unrequited love.

Finding That Special Someone

An Aries looking for love is less like a pioneer and more like a prospector, and the rule in prospecting is "Gold is where you find it." Capable of meeting a potential romantic interest practically anywhere and everywhere, Arians are always alert and not at all shy when on the lookout.

First Dates

An ideal first date for an Aries would be one where the Aries is in charge. On the perfect romantic excursion, the Aries' date would go wherever the Aries wanted to go and would do exactly what the Aries wanted to do! Since Arians like to be the first in everything, a movie premier, the opening of a new restaurant, or any place that has just opened would make a great setting for a night out. Arians like hot and spicy foods, so a Mexican or Indian restaurant would also be appropriate.

Aries in Love

The expression "All's fair in love and war" sums up Aries' approach perfectly. When it comes to love, Arians enjoy the chase and the challenge of overcoming obstacles as much as the conquest itself. They are not afraid to enter into a relationship with someone who is already involved with another person. Arians need an exciting partner who will never bore them—routine is the kiss of death for a love affair involving an Aries. Surprisingly, independent Aries needs more affection from a lover than any other sign in the zodiac.

Arians are attractive because of their natural energy. Excited by new challenges and experiences, Arians like to go on adventures with the one they love. They want their partner to be as interested and enthusiastic about their dreams and goals as they are.

Undying Love

Aries are less likely to settle down than people born under most signs. However, once they fall in love they do not second-guess themselves; they plunge in head-first and give it their all. They like to be completely enmeshed in their partner's life. The evolved Aries does this because he wants to help his lover succeed, while the less-evolved Aries will try to control his partner as a way to reduce the fear that this lover may do the wrong thing. Anyone who wants a relationship with

Aries to endure must let the Aries in. Everlasting passion is the hallmark of the long-term Aries relationship. Forever young, Arians work hard to balance the innocence of youth with the wisdom of years.

Expectations in Love

At all times and from all people, Aries expect honesty and passion. They also expect to be given the freedom to be themselves fully. But when in a loving relationship, this expectation becomes magnified tenfold, and nothing less than 100 percent of their lover's attention and devotion will do. Aries do not do well with partners who want to remain friends with former lovers. It's not that they're jealous; they simply expect that they will be all their lover needs and wants.

An Aries must be able to speak her mind forcefully, even if what she has to say is something that her partner or a prospective partner does not want to hear. She expects to be able to get angry and get over it quickly without her lover ever mentioning the experience again. Though highly aware of how strong and brave one must be to get by in life, Aries has a wonderful childlike quality and needs a lover with a sense of humor or who looks at things in a unique way.

What Aries Look For

Arians are looking for someone who is vibrant, positive, and authentic. They test everyone they're interested in, trying to find that special someone who is true to himself and not afraid of a strong partner—or anything else, for that matter. They'll endure both complexity and high drama to win a lover's affections, but once that battle is over, they will tolerate neither.

If Aries Only Knew...

If Aries only knew how brave they appear to be, they would never worry about having to put up an aggressive, overly confident front at the slightest feeling of self-doubt. Arians are so busy being their pure self that they don't realize that some consider them bossy. They don't crave power for its own sake; they simply are not comfortable when anything they are connected with is not clearly defined or resolved, and so they immediately take action to force all concerned to create a definite resolution.

Marriage

Aries wants a partner of whom she can be proud, yet a savvy partner would be wise to be modest about personal goals and to put effort into supporting those of the sensitive Aries. The person who becomes the spouse of a typical Aries must realize that the Aries will be quite happy to leave the day-to-day details to him but will want to be in control of all major decisions—starting with the wedding ceremony. Anyone who partners with an Aries can expect an exciting, stimulating, and creative relationship with plenty of affection and surprises. What's more, the Aries partner will always keep her word.

Aries' Opposite Sign

Libra, the Scales, is the opposite sign of Aries. Although relationships between Aries and Libra can sometimes be difficult, Libra can show Aries how to cooperate, share, and bring people together in harmony. Libra can intervene diplomatically, where Aries will charge in, forcibly making demands. Both signs are quite aggressive but for different reasons. Aries wants to get his way, while Libra wants peace and balance; both are willing to fight for what they believe.

Pairing Up

In general, if people display the characteristics typical of their sign, intimate relationships between an Aries and another individual can be described as follows:

Aries with Aries
Harmonious, with occasional brief but spectacular arguments

Aries with Taurus
Harmonious, as long as Aries is the boss

Aries with Gemini
Harmonious and in constant motion

Aries with Cancer
Difficult, because Aries has little patience for moodiness

Aries with Leo
Harmonious, with great achievements possible

Aries with Virgo
Turbulent in a romantic relationship, but good as friends

Aries with Libra
Difficult, but common goals and enemies can make it work

Aries with Scorpio
Turbulent and passionate in the extreme

Aries with Sagittarius
Harmonious, with the kind of honesty only they can endure

Aries with Capricorn
Difficult, because Aries feels restricted by Capricorn's dark side

Aries with Aquarius
Harmonious in the extreme; a mutual admiration society

Aries with Pisces
Harmonious if Pisces is willing to trust Aries to lead the way

If Things Don't Work Out

If Arians feel that they've been lied to or dishonored, there is the slightest of possibilities that they'll give a lover a second chance. However, if they've been humiliated, the relationship is over, and they never want to see the person who humiliated them again. Aries trust that they have the power to move on and start over. When an Aries has decided that she wants to go, there is no use trying to stop her.

Aries at Work

Aries do their jobs as if they own the company. This trait can manifest itself in several ways. Evolved Arians are willing to work until they drop to get the job done for the good of all. Others emulate the kind of owner who likes to have workers to boss around.

It is important that an Aries be able to work without too much interference or even supervision. Aries have the ability to work well with others, but they must be careful that they do not get distracted with the needs and goals of other people. They enjoy helping others to shine and can be content to share the glory with the group. But they mainly like to lead. Aries are goal oriented and will naturally formulate a plan for their own career advancement while immersed in the reality of their work. Aries are often impatient with the pace of others or with the speed at which they themselves are able to climb the ranks. However, they should avoid being too honest about that.

The innovative ideas of Aries are a rare commodity that must be valued and acted on immediately. Aries know they have something unique to contribute to any team, and if they are not allowed to do so, they will take their contribution elsewhere. Born explorers, they are interested in experiencing for themselves what is real, not simply accepting what other people say is real, and they will work tirelessly at anything they think is worth doing.

Typical Occupations

Aries like occupations where they can be free to exercise their creativity, imagination, and original approach to projects. They are great promoters and can accomplish a lot when faced with a short deadline. Publishing, publicity, advertising, and visual media production are natural professions for them to prevail in, as rapid decision making, a quick mind, and multiple skills are necessary attributes for these occupations.

Aries also excel as individual artists espousing a unique form of creative expression. They enjoy a job where initiative, intuition, inventiveness, energy, leadership qualities, and enthusiasm are required. The military, recruitment, training, and law enforcement are other fields that appeal to Aries. In a similar capacity, Aries make excellent surgeons and surgical nurses.

Aries are associated with positions that inspire activity in others. They gravitate to any position that has authority. Aries must be in command or they will lose interest. They work best at the beginning of a project, leaving the details and execution to other people.

Details, Details

Aries prefers not to have to take care of the details of a job, but will do so if necessary. Aries would much rather make lists and help everyone get started, then hand the job off to someone they trust. They need to be able to take full credit for the successes and be able to explain away the failures of anything with which they are connected. Some astrologers feel that Arians have a problem finishing what they've started, but this only happens when the ability to get full credit gets taken away from them.

Behavior and Abilities at Work

In the workplace, a typical Aries:

- displays contagious enthusiasm
- possesses the stamina to work long hours
- gets the job done early
- manifests loyalty and honesty
- takes an apolitical approach
- will quit if bored or unappreciated
- initiates ideas and concepts

Aries As Employer

A typical Aries boss:

- ✺ needs respect and loyalty
- ✺ calms down quickly if angered
- ✺ rewards hard work
- ✺ wants to see new, improved ways of doing things
- ✺ gets to the point quickly
- ✺ will do the job if subordinates fail to
- ✺ expects everyone to multitask

Aries As Employee

A typical Aries employee:

- ❀ looks for opportunities for advancement
- ❀ works best without close supervision
- ❀ can be careless with details and secrets
- ❀ comes up with original solutions
- ❀ isn't afraid of challenges or taking risks
- ❀ makes lists for herself and coworkers
- ❀ needs praise and other rewards

Aries As Coworker

Aries have the ability to anticipate what must be done and to do it without being told what to do. This makes them quite resistant to being directed by others. However, Aries will always be the first in line to volunteer. Aries have only two speeds, "off" and "on." When given the freedom to act on their instincts, they are willing to put their all into a project, even if it means working around the clock until the job is finished.

People who are insecure about their own capabilities may feel threatened by the display of Aries self-confidence, willpower, and ability. However, over time, when others see that the Aries' actions are not politically motivated, they will appreciate having such a dependable, uncompromising individualist on their team.

Money

Aries worry less about money than any other sign. They have no doubt that they'll be able to obtain enough money to get what they want. They seem blessed by fate with the ability to extricate themselves from financial problems using methods that others would overlook.

Many Arians are not comfortable with inherited wealth and may even work against their own interests by expending these resources faster than they can be replenished. They revel in any and all rewards that result from their own efforts or from ideas that are related to them personally. It is not unusual to find an Aries making money from an idea that arose from a personal experience or need, creatively translating it into something that can benefit both himself and others.

At Home

Arians always have several home improvement projects on their list. They must finish one before starting another or they will not finish any of them. They don't need much sleep, but they sleep well.

Behavior and Abilities at Home

Aries typically:

❄ gets annoyed easily if not permitted to "rule the roost"

❄ alternates between being totally busy and indulging in total relaxation

❄ dislikes feeling restricted

❄ spends money to make the home run smoothly

❄ will move if unable to feel secure at home for any reason

Leisure
Interests

Aries like to show off their prowess and competitive nature on both the physical and mental planes. They enjoy competitive sports, hiking, and camping. They also enjoy playing cards and participating in other games and activities that give them the opportunity to win.

The typical Aries enjoys the following pastimes:

* hobbies that involve metal tools or cutting, such carpentry, quilting, or collage

* physical activities that are done alone (not team sports)

* competitions

* martial arts

* adventure vacations

* home renovations

* watching others do things that the Aries is good at

Arian Likes

- 🌸 winning
- 🌸 handmade items
- 🌸 easy money
- 🌸 new clothes
- 🌸 red flowers
- 🌸 spicy foods
- 🌸 fast cars
- 🌸 surprise parties
- 🌸 instant gratification
- 🌸 one-of-a-kind gifts

Arian Dislikes

- being late
- restrictions
- losing
- feeling hungry
- being bested unfairly
- standing in line
- indecision
- phonies
- plain food

The Secret Side of Aries

Inside anyone who has strong Aries influences is a sweet, innocent, childlike soul who wishes she didn't have to fight so hard to get things to be the way she knows they have to be. Aries' forceful nature conceals a basic vulnerability that needs praise and affection from trusted loved ones to counter the often harsh words and deeds of others who find themselves the object of Aries' willful acts.

Mars ♂

The planet Mars rules the sign of Aries. Since ancient times, Mars has been thought of as "the angry red planet" and bears the name of the Roman god of war. Modern space explorations have revealed the planet to have a surface resembling one devastated by war.

But the fiery, hotheaded, quick-to-act image does not represent the complete astrological meaning of Mars. The planet represents willpower, the energy possessed by the ego that enables people to go after, gain, and accomplish what they want. Mars is how people assert themselves as individuals. Through Mars, one grows strong through challenge, competition, and debate and by being forced to confront the strength of personal desires and dedication. Mars rules the head and especially the face. He also rules weapons.

Like Mars, Aries is a "doer," a heroic inspiration to compatriots and a force to be reckoned with by the opposition. The energy of Mars helps Aries to accomplish goals without any personal compromise. If this energy is used for mindless, hostile aggression, Aries will quickly find that he is not the only one with strong desires.

Bringing Up a Young Aries

More than those born under almost any other sign, the Aries child needs to know that he is loved and valued. Despite the brave face Aries children put on, big hugs and constant reassurance are essential, especially after emotional bumps.

Young Arians must be helped to accept the fact that we all have limits and fears and that these, too, have a purpose—to keep us from doing things we should not be doing. If they are not successfully taught these lessons, there is the danger that fears will turn into phobias.

Aries youngsters will explore anything new to them in a cautious manner until they feel they understand it. Then they'll act as if they are experts and take risks inappropriate to their level of experience. Caregivers must continually expand the boundaries of what they're teaching an Aries child so there will be less of a tendency for the child to become a reckless know-it-all.

Simply saying "no" to an Aries child doesn't work, nor does persuasion or using other obedient kids as examples. Aries children of any age respond best to a challenge. Give an Aries child a test and he'll go into action, to prove he is better than anyone else—even if the test involves doing something he doesn't like.

The Aries Child

The typical Aries child:

❊ throws tantrums, but quickly recovers

❊ pays attention and wants attention

❊ has a competitive nature

❊ is capable of playing by himself

❊ displays a headstrong will

❊ studies in quick bursts

❊ has a loving and demonstrative nature

❊ is not afraid to do her own thing

❊ can have unusual phobias

Aries As a Parent

The typical Aries parent:

- plays like a kid
- gives a lot of appreciation and praise
- can create imaginative worlds
- can be abrupt and strict
- will raise children with good self-esteem
- may try to be controlling
- leaps to the defense of loved ones
- displays affection and generosity

Health

In astrology, Aries rules the head and the face. What's going on in an Aries' head—especially feelings of stress caused by fear of humiliation, missed deadlines, and lost opportunities—strongly influences what is going on in the body and makes Aries prone to headaches, toothaches, and unexplained neuralgia around the jaws. Arians can "burn out" from too much work. They're so busy, they haven't

got time to be sick,
but when they do fall ill, they
make a speedy recovery. Aries
need to be careful of doing things too
quickly, as they may injure themselves
with knives or scissors. They should take
care not to strain their eyes. Little "time
outs" are good for an Aries: hot baths,
five minutes in a hammock, a stroll in
the fresh air—these will work
wonders.

FAMOUS ARIES

Patricia Arquette

Johann Sebastian Bach

Alec Baldwin

Warren Beatty

Marlon Brando

Matthew Broderick

Charlie Chaplin

Joan Crawford

Russell Crowe

Leonardo da Vinci

Celine Dion

W.C. Fields

Al Green

Harry Houdini

Thomas Jefferson

Elton John

Eddie Murphy

Napoleon

Sarah Jessica Parker

Diana Ross

Gloria Steinem

Vincent van Gogh

Tennessee Williams

Reese Witherspoon

THE
ENCHANTED
WORLD
of
AMY ZERNER
&
MONTE FARBER

About the Authors

Internationally known self-help author Monte Farber's inspiring guidance and empathic insights impact everyone he encounters. Amy Zerner's exquisite one-of-a-kind spiritual couture creations and collaged fabric paintings exude her profound intuition and deep connection with archetypal stories and healing energies. Together, they have built The Enchanted World of Amy Zerner and Monte Farber: books, card decks, and

oracles that have helped millions discover their own spiritual paths.

Their best-selling titles include The Chakra Meditation Kit, The Enchanted Tarot, The Instant Tarot Reader, The Psychic Circle, Karma Cards, The Truth Fairy, The Healing Deck, True Love Tarot, Animal Powers Meditation Kit, The Breathe Easy Deck, The Pathfinder Psychic Talking Board, and Gifts of the Goddess Affirmation Cards.

For further information, please visit: **www.TheEnchantedWorld.com**